BROADWAY FAVORITES

Solos and Band Arrangements
~~correla~~ted with Essential Elements Band Method

Arranged by
MICHAEL SWEENEY

Welcome to Essential Elements Broadway Favorites! There are two versions of each selection in this versatile book. The SOLO version appears in the beginning of each student book. The FULL BAND arrangements of each song follows. The supplemental CD recording or PIANO ACCOMPANIMENT BOOK may be used as an accompaniment for solo performance. Use these recordings when playing solos for friends and family.

Solo Page	Band Arr. Page	Title	Correlated with Essential Elements
2	13	Beauty And The Beast	Book 1, page 19
3	14	Tomorrow	Book 1, page 19
4	15	Cabaret	Book 1, page 29
5	16	Edelweiss	Book 1, page 29
6	17	Don't Cry For Me Argentina	Book 2, page 14
7	18	Get Me To The Church On Time	Book 2, page 14
8	19	I Dreamed A Dream	Book 2, page 14
9	20	Go Go Go Joseph	Book 2, page 29
10	21	Memory	Book 2, page 29
11	22	The Phantom Of The Opera	Book 2, page 29
12	23	Seventy Six Trombones	Book 2, page 29

ISBN 978-0-7935-9855-7

HAL•LEONARD®
CORPORATION
7777 W. BLUEMOUND RD. P.O. BOX 13819 MILWAUKEE, WI 53213

From Walt Disney's BEAUTY AND THE BEAST: THE BROADWAY MUSICAL

BEAUTY AND THE BEAST

TUBA
Solo

Lyrics by HOWARD ASHMAN
Music by ALAN MENKEN
Arranged by MICHAEL SWEENEY

Play lower note if possible

From the Musical Production ANNIE

TOMORROW

Lyric by MARTIN CHARNIN
Music by CHARLES STROUSE
Arranged by MICHAEL SWEENEY

TUBA
Solo

From the Musical CABARET

CABARET

Words by FRED EBB
Music by JOHN KANDER
Arranged by MICHAEL SWEENEY

TUBA
Solo

From THE SOUND OF MUSIC
EDELWEISS

TUBA
Solo

Lyrics by OSCAR HAMMERSTEIN II
Music by RICHARD RODGERS
Arranged by MICHAEL SWEENEY

00860049

From EVITA
DON'T CRY FOR ME ARGENTINA

TUBA
Solo

Words by TIM RICE
Music by ANDREW LLOYD WEBBER
Arranged by MICHAEL SWEENEY

MCA Music Publishing

From MY FAIR LADY

GET ME TO THE CHURCH ON TIME

Words by ALAN JAY LERNER
Music by FREDERICK LOEWE
Arranged by MICHAEL SWEENEY

TUBA
Solo

00860049

From LES MISÉRABLES
I DREAMED A DREAM

Music by CLAUDE-MICHEL SCHÖNBERG
Lyrics by ALAIN BOUBLIL,
JEAN-MARC NATEL and HERBERT KRETZMER
Arranged by MICHAEL SWEENEY

TUBA
Solo

Music and French Lyrics Copyright © 1980 by Editions Musicales Alain Boublil
English Lyrics Copyright © 1986 by Alain Boublil Music Ltd. (ASCAP)
This edition Copyright © 1998 by Alain Boublil Music Ltd. (ASCAP)
Mechanical and Publication Rights for the U.S.A. Administered by Alain Boublil Music Ltd. (ASCAP)
c/o Spielman Koenigsberg & Parker LLP, Richard Koenigsberg, 1745 Broadway, New York NY 10019, Tel 212-453-2500, Fax 212-453-2550, ABML@skpny.com

00860049

From JOSEPH AND THE AMAZING TECHNICOLOR DREAMCOAT

GO GO GO JOSEPH

Music by ANDREW LLOYD WEBBER
Lyrics by TIM RICE
Arranged by MICHAEL SWEENEY

TUBA
Solo

Upper notes are optional

Upper notes are optional

From CATS
MEMORY

TUBA
Solo

Music by ANDREW LLOYD WEBBER
Text by TREVOR NUNN after T.S. ELIOT
Arranged by MICHAEL SWEENEY

Moderately Slow

00860049

From THE PHANTOM OF THE OPERA

THE PHANTOM OF THE OPERA

Music by ANDREW LLOYD WEBBER
Lyrics by CHARLES HART
Additional Lyrics by RICHARD STILGOE and Mike Batt
Arranged by MICHAEL SWEENEY

TUBA
Solo

00860049

From Meredith Willson's THE MUSIC MAN

SEVENTY SIX TROMBONES

TUBA
Solo

By MEREDITH WILLSON
Arranged by MICHAEL SWEENEY

BEAUTY AND THE BEAST

Lyrics by HOWARD ASHMAN
Music by ALAN MENKEN
Arranged by MICHAEL SWEENEY

TUBA
Band Arrangement

From the Musical Production ANNIE

TOMORROW

TUBA
Band Arrangement

Lyric by MARTIN CHARNIN
Music by CHARLES STROUSE
Arranged by MICHAEL SWEENEY

From the Musical CABARET
CABARET

TUBA
Band Arrangement

Words by FRED EBB
Music by JOHN KANDER
Arranged by MICHAEL SWEENEY

00860049

From THE SOUND OF MUSIC
EDELWEISS

TUBA
Band Arrangement

Lyrics by OSCAR HAMMERSTEIN II
Music by RICHARD RODGERS
Arranged by MICHAEL SWEENEY

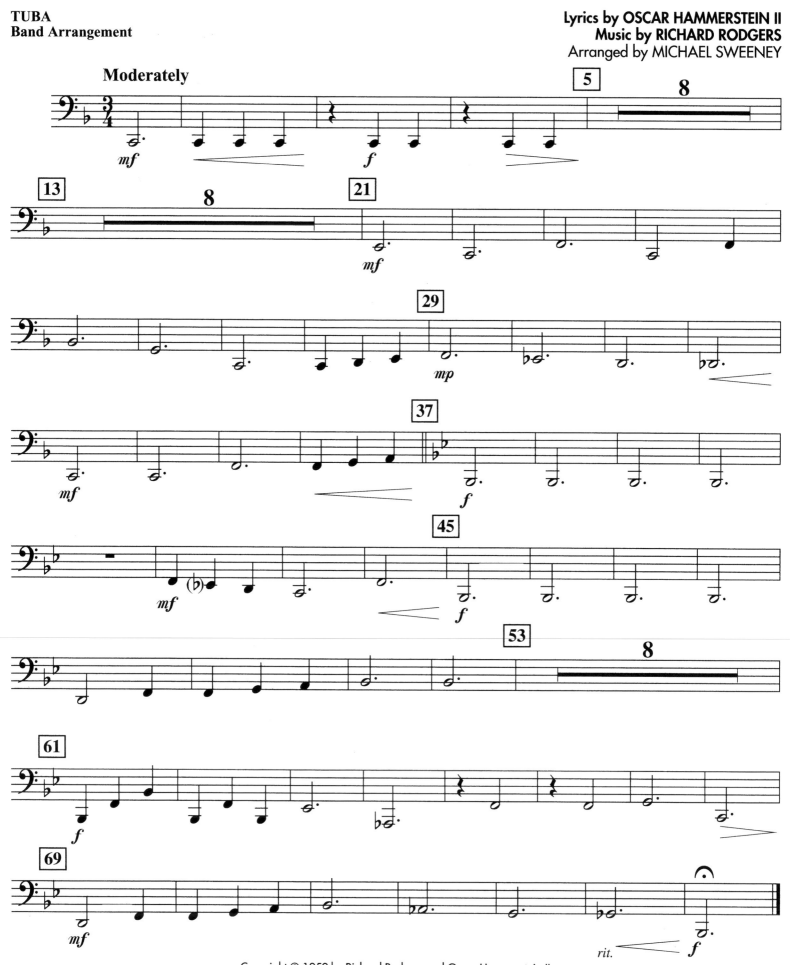

DON'T CRY FOR ME ARGENTINA

TUBA
Band Arrangement

Words by TIM RICE
Music by ANDREW LLOYD WEBBER
Arranged by MICHAEL SWEENEY

From MY FAIR LADY

GET ME TO THE CHURCH ON TIME

TUBA
Band Arrangement

Words by ALAN JAY LERNER
Music by FREDERICK LOEWE
Arranged by MICHAEL SWEENEY

00860049

I DREAMED A DREAM

TUBA
Band Arrangement

Music by CLAUDE-MICHEL SCHÖNBERG
Lyrics by ALAIN BOUBLIL,
JEAN-MARC NATEL and HERBERT KRETZMER
Arranged by MICHAEL SWEENEY

00860049

From JOSEPH AND THE AMAZING TECHNICOLOR DREAMCOAT
GO GO GO JOSEPH

TUBA
Band Arrangement

Music by ANDREW LLOYD WEBBER
Lyrics by TIM RICE
Arranged by MICHAEL SWEENEY

From CATS
MEMORY

TUBA
Band Arrangement

Music by ANDREW LLOYD WEBBER
Text by TREVOR NUNN after T.S. ELIOT
Arranged by MICHAEL SWEENEY

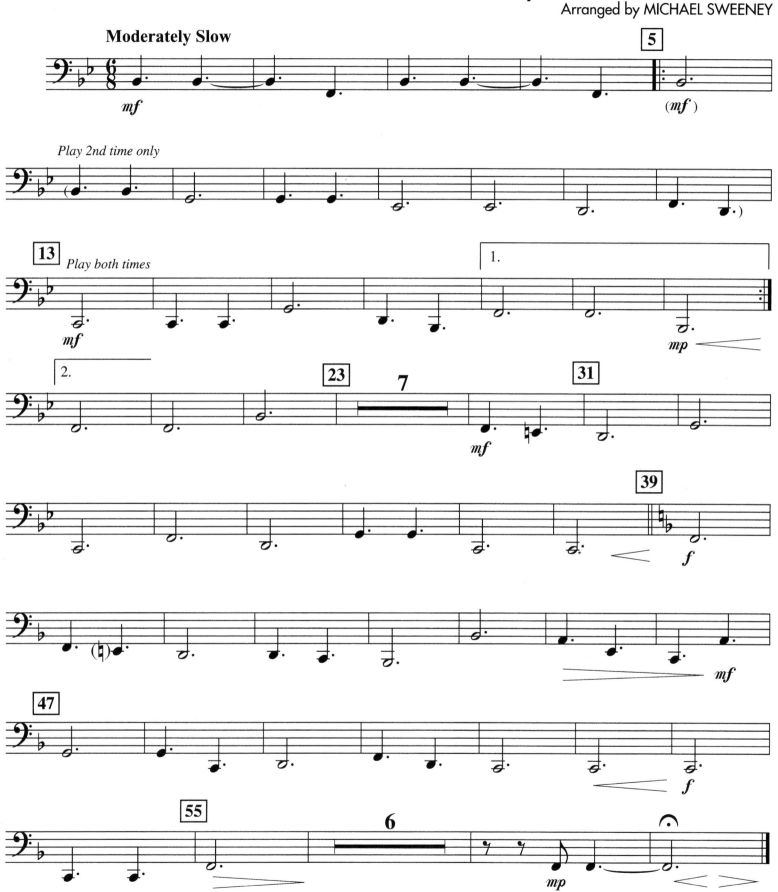

From THE PHANTOM OF THE OPERA

THE PHANTOM OF THE OPERA

TUBA
Band Arrangement

Music by ANDREW LLOYD WEBBER
Lyrics by CHARLES HART
Additional Lyrics by RICHARD STILGOE and MIKE BATT
Arranged by MICHAEL SWEENEY

From Meredith Willson's THE MUSIC MAN

SEVENTY SIX TROMBONES

By MEREDITH WILLSON
Arranged by MICHAEL SWEENEY

TUBA
Band Arrangement

00860049